Treasury of
French Dolls

Album 2

Lydia Richter

Treasury of
French Dolls
Album 2

HPBooks®

Publisher: Rick Bailey
Editorial Director: Randy Summerlin
Editors: Judith Schuler, David A. Silverman
Art Director: Don Burton
Book Assembly: Leslie Sinclair
Book Typography: Cindy Coatsworth, Michelle Claridge
Translation: Ruth A. Lewis and John S. Lewis
Technical Consultant: Mildred Seeley

HPBooks®
P.O. Box 5367
Tucson, AZ 85703
(602) 888-2150
ISBN: 0-89586-329-4
Library of Congress Catalog Card Number: 84-80436
© 1984 Fisher Publishing, Inc.
Printed in U.S.A.

Originally published in Germany as *Französische Porzellanpuppen: Puppen Album 2*.
©1981, 1983 by Verlag Laterna magica GmbH and Co.

Acknowledgments
For the loan of dolls and accessories, we wish to thank Miss Agnes Bögner, Miss Christiane Hermelink, Mrs. Roswitha Schaad, Mrs. Gabriele von Eicken and Mrs. Ulrike Zweig-Graefenhahn. Doll clothes from old material were made by Mrs. Margarete Schmidt and Mrs. Gertrud Stangl.
Editorial Collaboration and Technical Advice
Information on page 9 and pages 16 through 20 were written by Mrs. Dorothea Roth. Technical advice was provided by Mrs. Roswitha Schaad.
Photographs
All photographs by Joachim F. Richter, except pages 26, 27, 29, 33, 39, 48, 56, 57, 66, 73, 84, 85, which are by Hans Graf. Pages 8, 9, 11, 16, 20 are by Christiane Hermelink. Pages 28, 35, 38, 80 are by Lydia Richter.

Author Lydia Richter and her husband Joachim

TABLE OF CONTENTS

Bisque, Société Française de Fabrication
de Bébés et Jouets, or SFBJ, marked *No.
301, Paris 22.*
Made around 1915.

In Defense of Doll Collecting

Doll collecting is a fast-growing hobby. This relatively new pastime involves a subject that is lovable, interesting and almost human. But, strange as it may seem, even today there is prejudice and reserve regarding people who publicly confess they love and collect dolls.

Perhaps critics think people should no longer be interested in dolls. Or they may have had a negative experience with dolls when they were young. It could be critical comments made by uncomprehending contemporaries. Considering all the curiosities that have been found worthy of collecting, from objects as pedestrian as matchbook covers to those as extraordinary as the Tsar's Faberge eggs, the doll collector is assured of a lovable subject worth collecting.

It is easy to believe a collector can have a strong personal involvement with dolls. They have always been among the most tradition-rich, international toys available.

The love of collecting has a natural basis. When you collect dolls, you are not involved in an unusual or eccentric pastime. Instead, this hobby offers the charm of rich relationships. A doll's glowing red cheeks, gleaming eyes and luxurious hair are part of its charm. As a result, a doll preserves an ideal of beauty usually overlooked by playing children.

Dancing doll, named *Gisele*, on a music box, from a period catalog.

Mit der Puppe sitzt das Bertchen
Unterm Baum im Sonnenschein.
Da kommt Fritz mit seinem Pferdchen,
Spricht: „Was thust du hier allein?

Laß die Puppe, komm wir suchen
Uns den Reifen und den Ball;
Püppchen kriegt dann ein Stück Kuchen,
Und der Gaul kommt in den Stall."

Jester or farce doll, called a *Marotte*. Doll is fastened to a wood rod.

Dolls are present-day examples of a long-vanished era. They are a phenomenon of our cultural history whose worth can be judged only by adults. Collectors' dolls do not belong in children's hands, even though they can still make children's eyes gleam.

Even if a fascination with dolls cannot be explained, the charm of dolls can be explained by their beauty. Not all collectables are so thoroughly based on the charm, beauty and esthetics that a doll radiates. You can appreciate fine, delicately painted porcelain, an elegant hairstyle and lovely costume—they all add to the charm of the doll.

Knowledge that a doll was made and acquired by someone else serves to remind us that as collectors, we are caretakers. It is good to know we are helping to stop destruction and slow decay.

When you collect old dolls, you are not just building a collection. This hobby includes preserving old clothes and accessories, identification of different bodies, wigs, shoes and related items. It also deals with restoration of jewelry and other decorations. The entire scope of doll collecting gives you a feeling of joy and achievement.

Learn from Experience

When you begin to collect dolls, learning from experience may cost hundreds, even thousands, of dollars. The beginning collector views expensive dolls, pondering the devastating judgment of a doll expert who, unfortunately, was asked too late for advice.

A crack in a doll's head hidden beneath the wig, a baby head on a jointed body, plastic eyes or different legs—these are evident. Maybe after your purchase, you can still hear the assurances of the seller: "Original condition!" What can you do? Simply, learn from your mistakes.

Study Literature and Talk to Dealers

There are many ways to learn about dolls. Study specialized literature about dolls, such as books, price guides, doll catalogs and auction catalogs. These will give you a good perspective from the beginning. Make contact with other collectors. They may have encountered similar problems in their collecting. It is important to travel to doll shows, auctions and doll-club meetings.

Talk to dealers who can give you the benefit of their experience. In many large cities, there should be at least one dealer who will work with collectors and offer good advice. Often, collectors can get valuable information at auctions. With an auction catalog in hand, make a preliminary inspection of the dolls you are interested in. Learn about prices. For further information on dolls and tips on starting a doll collection, read HPBooks' *Doll Collecting for Fun & Profit*, by Mildred and Colleen Seeley.

In the Beginning

You may have decided you want to begin collecting dolls and are willing to travel in search of them. At first, visit only specialty stores. In the end, dolls you buy at a convenient flea market may be too expensive because you are not always sure of what you are getting.

Be wary of cracks in a bisque, china or parian head. A single crack greatly reduces the value of a doll. It is important for a doll to be in original condition. For example, the head must go with the body. This is easy to judge, based on a comparison of the head and body size. Unfortunately, dolls are often assembled from mismatched pieces. It is not uncommon to find a German doll head with a French body. This mixup is a serious violation of style. You may also find one arm bigger than the other or made of different materials. These inconsistencies can occur in many different forms. Flaws will generally decrease the price.

Often, older dolls do not have their original wig. For dolls with damaged or missing hair, there are beautiful new human-hair wigs, which often completely change the appearance of a doll. The most beautiful original wigs were made of mohair, which is wool from the Angora goat. A doll should wear its hair in the fashion of its own time, but unfortunately this is rare today.

Many old dolls had handblown glass eyes. However, plastic eyes can be found because dolls were taken to "doll clinics" for repair. If the repair person did not have glass eyes available—they have not been made since about 1930—he probably used unbreakable plastic. If you have acquired a doll with plastic eyes, it is essential to change the eyes to glass.

Types of Collections

One important criterion is the choice of the specialty or type of doll to collect. You may choose parian dolls, bisque dolls, character dolls, baby dolls or mechanical dolls. It is important to make your decision early.

Perhaps your heart yearns for wood-and-wax dolls. Do you want dolls of each type? Where do you begin? Where do you stop? How well prepared are you to give up other things? These are questions you must consider carefully.

Bisque, maker unknown, 26-3/4 inches (68cm), marked *B12M*. Made around 1880, doll has characteristic *Bébé Mothereau* body. Composition torso body has wood upper arms and ball-and-socket joints. Feet are unusually small.

Bisque, Rostal, 22-3/4 inches (58cm). Made around 1890, swivel-head doll is called *Mon Trésor*, which means *my treasure*.

China, Parian and Bisque

Porcelain dolls were first made about 130 years ago. Porcelain, called *white gold*, was invented in 1710 by Böttger, a Dresden pharmacist and alchemist. More than 130 years passed before someone thought of using the material for making dolls. This creative idea may have been the result of an inventive doll maker or one of the royal workshops. However it came about, porcelain became the material for artistic figurines and elegant knickknack dolls.

According to records, porcelain doll heads were first displayed at the Vienna Trade Exposition of 1845. Lippert and Haas made them in collaboration with the Schlaggenwald porcelain factory. Others believe royal workshops, such as those in Berlin, Nymphenburg and Meissen, introduced handmade doll heads at the same time. Documentation is not available. These were the first factories to undertake large-scale production of doll heads that have been able to survive for posterity.

China

China-head dolls, called *glazed porcelain*, were the first dolls to be produced of the new material. Early, highly glazed, hard porcelain heads are distinguished by their molded hair, which was usually black. This was followed by dolls with tightly curled locks. This hairstyle was the dominant fashion during the early Victorian period. Following that, combed-back hairdos with buns or spirals over the ears were popular.

Around 1860, the beautiful "waterfall" or bun hairstyle was fashionable. After 1890, hair was styled in bangs. Hairstyle is usually a reliable indicator of the time or origin of a doll. This is especially true because hair fashions changed more slowly than women's clothing styles.

Soon, doll heads were not the only doll parts made of porcelain. Porcelain limbs, such as lower legs and forearms, were made next. The porcelain doll had arrived. By the middle of the century, the popularity of porcelain dolls began to overtake wood-jointed dolls. Porcelain dolls with fabric bodies became known as *Nanking dolls*.

Parian

Variations of porcelain were introduced. An unglazed, uncolored porcelain was called *parian*, after the famous marble of Paros, which it resembled. Parian was introduced in 1842 by Copeland in Staffordshire, England. Minton, another firm located there, was noted for producing parian.

A classic characteristic of parian dolls is their molded blond hair. Because black was poorly suited to the bright gloss of parian, you rarely find parian dolls with black or dark hair.

Bisque

During the brief popularity of parian heads, shiny porcelain heads evolved into mat-textured, lifelike bisque. Bisque has a silky-textured surface, which offered parian dolls lively competition. Bisque dolls had a peach-colored skin tone, oversized eyes and small open or closed mouths. It is usually thought that the first bisque head dolls were made between 1860 and 1870 in France, but there is no conclusive evidence.

Through those years, in Paris and Limoges and in Germany, bisque dolls were being made. In addition, bisque dolls with composition, leather or fabric bodies, half-dolls and all-bisque dolls were being made.

China, probably French, 19-3/4 inches (50cm).
Made from 1840 to 1850. Red hair is painted on bald head. Holes are located on sides, front and back of head for attaching wig. Cloth body has porcelain lower arms and legs.

Parian, probably by Gaultier, 9-3/4 inches (25cm).
Made around 1860, rare parian shoulder head has pink cheeks. Painted blue eyes have light-gray rays and black eyebrows. Mouth is closed. Hair is painted black. Cloth body has leather arms. Costume is original.

Doll Bodies

Bisque dolls usually had composition, leather or cloth bodies. Because there are many different doll bodies, pay special attention to the head to see if it is attached to its original body.

By 1869, French doll maker Bru had invented and patented his ball-and-socket jointed body. This made possible movement of joints in all directions.

Ten-jointed Jumeau child doll, shown in a costume on pages 62 and 63, demonstrates her versatility with different poses.

Also typical was the Jumeau body, shown above. Joints are cumbersome, and upper thighs can bend diagonally to the kneecap. Doll bodies of leather, cloth or similar materials were called *doll bags*. They were stuffed with many materials, including sawdust, seaweed and horsehair. Doll bodies are described in more detail on pages 24 and 25.

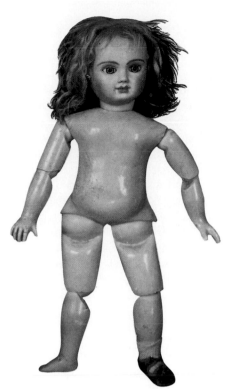

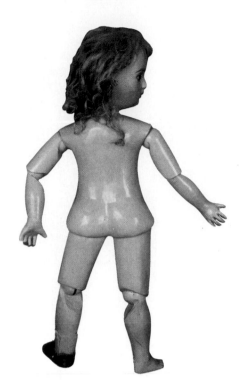

Left and Right: *Bébé Mothereau* has wood-composition body, wood upper arms and ball-and-socket joints. Feet are unusually small.

Below: Jumeau doll body has gold-medal marking and rare wool wig. Composition ball-and-socket jointed body has eight wood ball-joints.

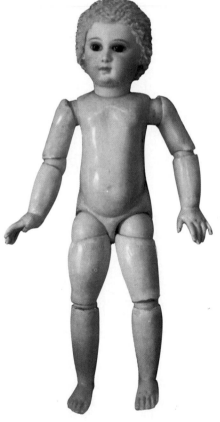

Left: French kid-leather body has gussets at arm and leg joints, and stitched leather hands.

Right: Molded fingernails are featured in detailed finish work on hand of Steiner *Le Parisien*.

Automatic, Semiautomatic and Mechanical Dolls

Supple leather-laced shoes

Old doll's purse made of leather, shown life-size

Doll's copper bottle warmer measures 2-1/2-inches (6-1/2cm) and was made around 1900

Action Dolls

The age of automatic dolls began with the discovery of balance wheels and steel springs. Technical applications of these were used in the doll industry. As early as 1743, Madeleine Cochin's engraving, *Mademoiselle Catherina*, shows an action doll being admired. The action doll was made by Pierre Gautier in 1764 and still exists. It is moved by a compression spring on a toothed wheel and wheeled undercarriage.

Charles Bruguin of London constructed an action doll around 1815. The doll could put one foot in front of the other. An American named Morrison called this action doll the *self-moving girl*. Designer A.V. Newton obtained a patent for it in 1862 in England. In 1855, Steiner of Paris caused a stir with his patent for an action doll. Although action dolls using hoisting mechanisms had been made for a long time, some doll companies introduced simpler mechanical walking dolls around the beginning of the 1900s. By manually moving the legs, these dolls' heads also moved.

Talking Dolls

Talking dolls had been developed by the 18th century, beginning in a way similar to action dolls. At first, the dolls could only squeak or scream. Johannes Mälzel successfully created a doll that could say "mama" and "papa" through the use of a bellows. Further development of talking and musical dolls, especially by Jumeau, was a result of Thomas Edison's invention of the phonograph in 1877. Equipment built into a doll body produced singing or playing of a song and speaking of words.

From Piano Playing to Hand Kissing

Jean Roullet established his company in 1865 and was joined by his son-in-law around 1880. The company, Roullet & Decamps, became the best-known maker of automatic dolls. They made the mechanism used in the *Marquis Fumeur* on pages 96 to 99.

Dolls from the Roullet & Decamps workshop could smoke, pick cherries, play the piano, play the violin, cast spells, tell fortunes and much more. Beginning in 1845, Paris-based Jean Rousselot built three-wheeled bases for action dolls, but they never reached the perfection of Roullet & Decamps' products.

In 1867, Bru patented a two-faced mechanical doll, called *Surprise Doll*. Later, German firms produced three- and five-faced dolls. German maker Carl Bergner made a doll with three faces—one laughing, one crying and one sleeping. It is shown in HPBooks' *Treasury of German Dolls: Album 1*, also by Lydia Richter. To change from one facial expression to another, a wood dowel protruding from the head is turned. In 1869, Bru patented his fully movable jointed dolls.

Competition was stiff among French manufacturers in the mechanical or automatic doll market. For example, Bru's dolls could drink and breathe. Jumeau countered with eating dolls and ones that could make music. Around 1880, Simon & Halbig of Germany created a sensation with a swimming doll, *Ondine*, which E. Martin of Paris had patented in 1876. *Ondine* had a small porcelain head attached to a cork body. In the body was a spring mechanism that caused the doll to make swimming movements with its arms and legs.

The collection of automatic and mechanical dolls knew no limits. It included such charming versions as Simon & Halbig's *Kusshandwerfende Puppe*, which means *kissing doll*, made around 1900.

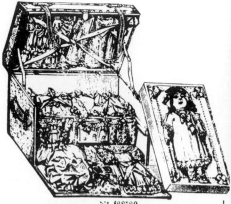

Large wardrobe, shown on top, and
small one, shown above, are from an
old catalog

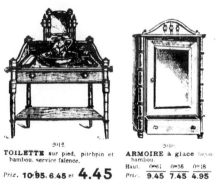

Catalog illustrations for mirror table,
wardrobe and four-poster bed

Some dolls came with a trousseau that included a trunk with dresses, corsets, hats and
other accessories.

Doll Clothing

The first French bisque dolls were *fashion dolls*, which were dressed in the
newest fashions. Fashion dolls were used to carry styles around the world. Later,
child dolls were popular and dressed according to current children's fashions.

Finding old doll costumes in the correct style of the day is a challenge for doll
collectors. A doll dressed in its original costume is rare if it is more than 100
years old. Not every doll was guarded in a glass case or sheltered from moths
and other pests.

If you cannot sew or do not understand tailoring, buy old fabric, lace and other
materials at flea markets and take them to a professional seamstress. You may
be able to find a doll seamstress who can dress the doll to perfection. Old
patterns, illustrations and reproduction catalogs make it possible to make a dress
today that is close to the original. It is worthwhile to pay attention to details. For
example, in the case of French bisque dolls, Jumeau dolls were dressed different-
ly from Bru dolls. For detailed information on dressing French and German
bisque dolls, read HPBooks' *Doll Costuming*, by Mildred and Colleen Seeley.

Typical among Jumeau doll costumes after 1880 was a long waist, with a little
skirt covering only the knee. Skirts were usually pleated or folded and were
about 1/3 the length of the costume. The top was elaborately decorated with
drawn lace or silk inserts. Collars were large or small, pointed or round.

Bru dresses often had long jackets with small pleated skirts. Most were
decorated with lace. The complete costume was usually lined with gauze or stiff
linen so the skirt stood out.

2001. BÉBÉ riche entièrement articulé, pouvant se déshabiller, costume satin rose, bleu et rouge.

Hauteur.	0m53	0m48	0m41
Prix.	**17.50**	**14.50**	**10.50**

Original Jumeau hat

2003. BÉBÉ entièrement articulé costume riche, dentelle.

Hauteur.	0m46	0m37
Prix.	**4.95**	**2.95**

Original Bru dress

2006.

Above and far right: Five catalog illustrations of old French doll clothes.

2007. BÉBÉ réclame demi-articulé, costume mode, bleu rose, rouge.

Hauteurs	0m45	0m36
Prix . . .	**2.95**	**1.45**

Old doll shoes with stamped decoration and red decorative stitching

DOLL A LA WATTEAU

B
R
U

BRU. J^{NE} R

Bru (Bru Jne. & Co.) of Paris and
Montreuil-sous-Bois made bisque dolls
from 1866 to 1899. Bru dolls are
recognized by their strong expressions.
Collectors value them because of their
beauty, especially baby dolls. Casimir
Bru patented ball-and-socket joint in
1869.

**Bisque, Jumeau, 24-1/2 inches
(62cm), marked _9 EJ._**
Made around 1880, swivel-head doll's
body is marked with gold medal. Ears
are mounted. Doll wears wool wig.
Early composition ball-and-socket
jointed body has eight wood joints.

**Bisque, Jumeau, 20-1/2 inches
(52cm).**
Made around 1885, swivel-head doll
has glass sleep eyes with cloth lashes.
See page 62 for more information on
doll.

16

Important French Doll Makers

Bru

The Bru Co., located in Paris, was at the top of the list of French doll makers.
Founded in 1866, Bru was the first doll manufacturer to be established on the
Rue Saint Denis. Other doll makers later located there. Bru was famous because
of his beautiful dolls. Early Bru dolls featured beautifully formed, exceptionally
delicate molded heads. These dolls had a slightly raised bust.

Bodies of the earliest Brus were goatskin. Their lower arms were made of
bisque and had beautiful hands. No other doll hands compare in quality to those
of Bru dolls. Lower legs were usually made of wood.

Early Bru dolls were not always marked. _BS_ possibly stands for dolls of this
type and origin. The earliest examples of Bru dolls were marked with a deeply
notched circle with a dot, as illustrated above left. You may also find a dot with a
half-moon. More frequently, the label _B Jne. & Cie._ is found on the back part of
the shoulder. _E. Déposé_ was engraved on the front. In 1898, because French
companies worked together, many Bru dolls were marked more than once.

The result is that genuine dolls might have a Jumeau-marked body with a Bru-
marked head. When Bru joined SFBJ, Société Française de Fabrication de Bébés
et Jouets, the companies no longer produced bisque or porcelain heads
themselves. It became less expensive to import pieces from Germany than to
make their own. In the meantime, they did not change the long-used French
neck mark. They gave commissions and remained designers and trendsetters.

Most early Brus—the "baby-doll" type was a child between 8 and 12 years
old—wore wigs made of Russian wool or mohair. These are found only occasionally today. They are delicate and must often be replaced by sturdier wigs.

Because it is stuffed with small pieces of cork, a doll may sit crooked and
stooped. This is in marked contrast to immovable wood limbs. To alleviate this
problem, immovable limbs were replaced by carved-wood lower legs and
forearms. These were attached by joints at the knees and elbows. After 1873,
this type of doll was able to move and sit naturally.

Later Bru dolls were made with a jointed wood body and a bisque swivel head.
Most Bru baby dolls had _open-closed mouths_, but there is no opening into the
head. Other Bru dolls had open or closed mouths. With their big round eyes and
soft lamb's-wool wigs, Bru baby dolls pleased children.

Original clothing of Bru dolls was hand sewn and looked like a work of art.
Dresses were made of velvet, silk, lace or the finest wool. Bru clothed child dolls
in the style of the time in which they were made. They can be regarded as miniature examples of courtly children's styles. As a result, when in original clothes,
Bru baby dolls can be dated by the style of their clothes.

Bru is regarded as the most exclusive French doll maker. When they were
new, Bru dolls commanded a high price. They were available only to the
wealthy.

Although early Bru dolls were charming, the company did not stagnate.
Technical improvements made dolls more movable, taking into account the
demand for more mobility. The 1881 model, _Bébé Gourmand_, which means
greedy baby, had a pullstring in the back of the head. This allowed it to eat and
swallow. _Bébé le Dormeur_, which means _sleeping baby_, had closing eyelids. Inno-
vations such as there were made at the expense of the doll's original beauty. Because of this, and despite their quality, dolls did not win higher than a silver
medal at toy exhibitions. The silver medal was awarded solely for clothing.

This situation did not change until Bru was taken over by H. Chevrot in 1883.
The company's name was changed to _Bru Jne. & Cie._, which means Bru Junior
and Co. Under Chevrot's leadership, Bru dolls brought home many gold medals.
Fancy original costumes covered inexpensive underwear, which was rarely seen
because dresses were long. After 1885, clothes covered the knees.

F. 8 G

Inscription of Gaultier of St. Maurice/Seine and Paris, 1860 to 1916. Company produced high-quality bisque doll heads.

JUMEAU   DÉPOSÉ
MEDAILLE d'OR   E. 7 J.
PARIS

Photo above: Roullet & Decamps made the smoking mechanism for Jumeau's Smoking Marquis. Made around 1890, the doll actually smokes. See pages 96 to 99.

Inscription above of one well-known doll maker, Jumeau of Paris and Montreuil-sous-Bois, from 1842 to 1899 (1899 to 1925 in SFBJ). Characteristics of Jumeau bisque heads, including baby dolls, are fascinating eyes and detailed painting.

Close-up photo shows apparatus in the Smoking Marquis. Mechanism includes springs and rods for moving head and arms, and bellows for inhaling and exhaling smoke.

Gaultier

François Gaultier's Paris doll workshop was famous for its mature *fashion doll* model, which was marked *F.G.* Older models of F.G. dolls can be recognized because the F.G. is surrounded by an elegant scroll. Dolls' heads are beautiful and made of the finest bisque. They were round and faces looked more mature than usual. Heads were bought by the Gaultier company from another manufacturer. Bodies came from Gaultier's workshop. The marking *F.G.* does not indicate this.

Turning heads with the marks of Jumeau and others have been found on Gaultier bodies. Dolls were beautifully costumed. However, costumes do not reflect children's clothing. They were copies of adult outfits.

Most Gaultier heads were designed as swivel heads and were attached to leather bodies. Arms and legs were made of leather. François Gaultier embodies in dolls called *Parisiennes* the splendid times of luxurious middle-class life. These were not toy dolls as much as enrichments of a lifestyle. Handmade costumes matched the high quality of beautiful bisque heads. The Gaultier company specialized in porcelain.

This company also contributed to improving the reputation of French dolls. Because F.G. dolls were rare, they commanded a high price, especially early models with closed mouths.

Recent research has uncovered new information regarding the French doll-making company, *Gaultier*. The founder, François Gaultier, originally spelled his last name *Gauthier*. He changed the spelling in 1875. This book uses the name François Gaultier.

Some books refer to *Ferdinand* or *Fernand* Gaultier, but no such doll maker existed. Confusion about Gaultier's first name resulted from errors made by researchers prior to the mid-1960s.

Definitive research that has cleared the name confusion of the Gaultier Co. was done by Florence Poisson, conservator of the Musée Roybet-Fould in Courbevoie, France. The results of her work were published in 1982 in Bulletin No. 7 of the Centre d'Étude et de Recherche sur les Poupées in Courbevoie.

Jumeau

Some of the most beautiful bisque dolls are Jumeau dolls. The Jumeau Co. was founded in 1840 and was entered into the Paris business registry that same year by Pierre François Jumeau and M. Belton. In the 1851 London World Exposition, their extravagantly costumed dolls caused an international sensation with the newest, most luxurious tailoring.

Until 1873, Jumeau doll heads were made by other companies. In 1873, Jumeau founded a factory with a porcelain oven in Montreuil. Despite coarse, carelessly worked bodies, Jumeau's finely cast, beautifully painted heads succeeded in winning a gold medal at the 1878 World Exhibition. Jumeau-marked heads with a soulful Jumeau expression and distinctive, fascinating glass enameled eyes, were mounted on wood-and-metal bodies covered with leather or tricot. In England, this type of Parisian doll was called *almond-eyed.*

Emile Jumeau was the youngest son of the company's founder. He occupied himself with improving the quality of the dolls, and under his leadership new doll heads were introduced. One example is the *Bébé Jumeau* of 1879. This was followed by another *Bébé Jumeau* in 1885, with eyelids that closed and a ball-jointed body.

The bisque of Jumeau dolls was especially fine. Costumes, which had been extravagant during the 1870s and 1880s, were not as distinguished in the 1890s. *Roi de Poupées*, which means king of dolls, was a title Emile Jumeau gave himself in 1894. But Jumeau could not hide the fact that the company was no longer as careful in its manufacturing, despite many technical improvements. Until the turn of the century, Jumeau was the only large French doll-making company using

Jullien
1

Jullien of Paris made dolls from 1863 to 1904. Baby dolls, mignonettes and jesters were made from 1892. *Bébé L'Universel*, which means Universal Baby, is a talking, walking doll with sleep eyes. It was introduced in 1895.

Inscription of Unis France, from 1922 to 1925. Bisque head made by SFBJ was not distinctive.

Inscription of Mme. Marie Antoinette Leontine Rohmer of Paris, doll maker from 1857 to 1880. The company made china and bisque dolls, which are well-known and treasured fashion dolls.

Déposé Jumeau, marked *DEP 8*. Made around 1890.

assembly-line production techniques. As German products entered the world market, the Jumeau Co. merged with eight other domestic doll and toy factories, including the Gaultier porcelain factory. They formed the *Société Française de Fabrication de Bébés et Jouets, SFBJ*, which means French Society for the Manufacture of Baby Dolls and Toys. Later, Jumeau dolls appeared with heads by Simon & Halbig.

Production of Jumeau dolls spanned a range of 14 sizes, up to about 40 inches (1m). After the Parisiennes, or fashion dolls, *model dolls* and especially *baby dolls*, with oversized eyes and childlike faces, contributed most to the company's reputation. At first, Jumeau concentrated on making shoulder heads with goatskin bodies over wire frames. Among Jumeau's later dolls, bisque heads were combined with jointed, composition bodies.

In retrospect, we can see that Jumeau was not idle regarding other technical details. The company experimented with heads, torsos and limbs. The best designers from the art and fashion worlds worked in an effort that became more refined. Eventually, Jumeau achieved such a reputation that the company could no longer be compared to any other doll maker. Jumeau then conquered America, with exhibitions in Philadelphia and New Orleans.

When Buffalo Bill and his Wild West Circus visited Paris in 1887, Jumeau presented him with the most beautiful Jumeau doll, the *Jumeau Triste*, which means the *sad Jumeau*. This doll was then called the *Cody-Jumeau* after William Cody, the real name of Buffalo Bill. It was also known as the *Long-Face Jumeau*.

After SFBJ's founding at the turn of the century, the Jumeau dynasty lost its exalted place. The company attempted a comeback while within SFBJ, showing twin dolls with unbreakable bodies in England. The twin dolls played on the meaning of the French word *jumeau*—twin. These dolls were expensive. The world-famous Jumeau doll company never regained its earlier fame, and the king of dolls was dethroned.

The term *DEP Jumeau* was used for any doll with a Jumeau body that was marked only with *DEP*, made between 1890 and 1910. Heads were made by German companies under subcontract with Jumeau. Although there is uncertainty regarding the identities of these companies, Simon & Halbig was the main supplier of these beautiful doll heads. DEP Jumeaus can often be identified by their finely molded, rippled eyebrows and sharp teeth. These dolls had pierced ears, which was not common among German dolls.

Heads were made under commission of Jumeau and later for SFBJ. They were provided with French bodies in France, where they were dressed and often packed in boxes labeled *Original Jumeau*. This was done for financial reasons because a DEP Jumeau could be sold for a lower price. Imported DEP heads were less expensive to make when compared with Jumeau heads made in France. The *Original Jumeau* stamp was not placed on these dolls by the firm, even though these were often beautiful dolls. DEP Jumeaus seldom achieved the high level of quality of the original Jumeau doll.

If you acquire a doll that has an original Jumeau body and a head with a DEP neck mark, it is a strong indication it is a *DEP Jumeau*.

Steiner

Although the name Steiner is German, Jules Nicholas Steiner was French. He allied himself with established French doll manufacturers in 1885. A clockmaker by profession, Steiner specialized in mechanical dolls. He patented a walking doll in 1855 and in 1890 produced an automatic walking doll that he called Baby's First Step. When the doll was wound, she moved her head, raised and lowered her arms, and moved her legs forward and backward to walk. A mechanical voice furthered the illusion that this was a tiny, living child walking on unsteady feet. This doll differed substantially from the first French walking doll made in 1826.

There was a walking Steiner, a crying Steiner and other dolls with lever mechanisms. The mechanism was located over the ears, and it controlled the eyes. Steiner dolls looked strikingly different from each other. In addition to being expressive, they differ in quality. Many doll faces have upper and lower

Ste F 3/0

Le Petit Parisien
BEBE STEINER

STEINER
.S.G.D.G.
PARIS
A11

Three neck marks of Jules Nicholas Steiner and Société Steiner of Paris. They made dolls from 1855 to 1891. This was a respected doll mark for bisque heads and walking dolls. Company created the baby doll, including the *Phénix Bébé* and others.

Déposé Jumeau, marked *DEP 3*. Made around 1900.

teeth. Their most exceptional feature is their pate. It is not made of cork, as is standard for other French manufacturers. Steiner pates were papier-mâché dyed purple. Steiner dolls' hands and feet have long fingers and toes, with a big toe that is not joined to the others.

With Steiner dolls, a trademark is often missing from his earliest dolls, which have pink shading above the eyes. Many Steiner dolls are marked with the name *Le Parisien* or sometimes *Bourgoine*. An entire series of Steiner dolls bears the mark *A*, followed by a number. These are called the *Steiner A Series*, and are noteworthy for their similarity to a certain Jumeau doll. A typical feature of the A series is long, dark eyelashes that begin in the corners of the eyes.

Société Française de Fabrication de Bébés et Jouets — SFBJ

In 1899, a number of French doll makers, most of whom had been successfully productive by themselves for many years, founded a joint manufacturing company that created a sensation. The *Société Française de Fabrication de Bébés et Jouets*, which means *French Society for the Manufacture of Baby Dolls and Toys*, was known by the initials SFBJ. Its formation was considered necessary because of increased competitive pressure from the German doll industry. Individual doll parts could be obtained easily from a Thuringian manufacturer and assembled in SFBJ's factories in Paris and Montreuil-sous-Bois. Dolls were marked with the letters *SFBJ*, but often the neck mark of an individual doll maker, now merged with the SFBJ, was also included. Some famous SFBJ manufacturers were Jumeau, Bru, Fleischmann & Bloedel, Rabery & Delphieu and Pintel & Godchaux.

Most of the dolls made by SFBJ had composition bodies, bisque heads and human-hair wigs. Glass eyes were round, and the whites of the eyes were visible beneath.

Beginning in 1905, SFBJ became a recorded trademark. In 1911, SFBJ produced three distinct doll creations, the *Bébé Prodige*, *Bébé Jumeau* and *Bébé Français*. About 5 million SFBJ dolls were made in 1912 and assembled by workers in Vincennes and Paris.

When World War I started, the companies were forced to reconsider their alliance and separated again into individual production units. The company known as SFBJ discontinued production.

After the war, the advantage of united production was once again considered, and work proceeded with new trademarks. In 1920, a small ring, or leg mark, was added under the shoes or wig.

Jumeau produced dolls from 1842 to 1899. Jumeau's yearly production in 1884 amounted to 220,000 pieces. The company put aside its own name when SFBJ was founded. While part of the alliance, it produced Jumeau-marked dolls based on old models, because the company's manufacturing plant in Montreuil-sous-Bois was used by the newly established SFBJ. As a result, it was not hard to include the old models in the new combination French-German dolls.

Bru also gained by its association with SFBJ. Fleischmann & Bloedel, originally from Germany, made a name in 1898 with their *Bébé Triomphe* in 1898, shortly before the formation of SFBJ. The Rabery & Delphieu company was founded in 1856 and taken over by Genty around 1898 or 1899. The company became known after 1875 for dolls with fixed or movable limbs on a wood body, and pink and white goatskin leather bodies. After 1890, the trademark *R.D.* stood for speaking, unbreakable jointed baby dolls. In 1893, the company received a patent for action and speaking dolls. It brought out *Bébé de Paris* in 1898. In 1899, Rabery & Delphieu joined SFBJ.

Other French Doll Makers

Dolls were made by other French doll-making companies. Even though the dolls were not made by Jumeau, Gaultier or Bru, they still display the good taste and excellent craftsmanship that French doll manufacturers are known for.

DÉPOSÉ.
S.F.B.J.

See page 19 for explanation of SFBJ.

Bisque character doll, SFBJ, 15-3/4 inches (40cm), marked *SFBJ 238*. Made around 1915, doll has composition ball-jointed body.

Bisque, Lanternier, 19-3/4 inches (50cm), marked *Déposé Fabrication française Favorite No.8 J.E. Masson sc Al & Cie.* Made around 1915, swivel-head doll has composition body.

Lanternier, of Limoges, made bisque heads from 1855 to 1925. Known inscriptions are *Favorite, La Georgienne* and *Lorraine*.

Denamur

Denamur Co. operated in Paris from 1857 to 1898. Emile Denamur manufactured a less-expensive E.D.-labeled doll for a larger market. It had molded teeth and pierced ears. Today, these dolls are easily confused with those by E. Dumont, Jumeau, Roullet and Decamps or Steiner.

Huret, Maison

Another company, Huret, Maison, was established in Paris from 1850 to 1920. It made jointed dolls of all kinds with porcelain heads after 1851. Huret, Maison obtained a patent in 1861 for a doll head that could move in all directions. They made lady dolls with wood bodies and metal hands. Huret dolls are recognized by their broad jawbone and double chin.

Jullien

Jullien Jeune was another French doll company. It existed in Paris from 1863 to 1904. Until 1875, the neck mark *JJ* was used on dressed babies and for Zouave dolls and puppets.

Jullien was known for its hand puppets that were sold for use in puppet theaters. From 1885, the company offered simple, unbreakable dressed baby dolls. In 1892, Jullien made four different types of *Bebe l'Universel*: stiff, jointed, speaking and beautifully dressed dolls. In 1895, Jullien produced an action *Bébé l'Universel* that had teeth, spoke and could move its eyes.

LeComte & Alliot and Lanternier, A. & Co.

Mainly mechanical dolls were offered by Lecomte & Alliot, which existed in Paris from 1866 to 1900. This company used the mark *L.C.*

Founded in Limoges in 1855, Lanternier, A. & Co. was originally a porcelain manufacturer. The company made its own beautiful bisque heads. Dolls, with names like *Favorite, La Georgienne* and *Lorraine*, were marked *A.L.* or *AL & Cie*. Around 1912, they made *Bébé Limoges*.

May Brothers & Co. and Mme. Rohmer

May Brothers & Co. of Paris existed from 1887 to 1897 and folded before SFBJ was founded. The company is known for *Bébé Mascotte*, which created a sensation in 1892. It was a jointed doll with knees that could be set in many positions. Surprisingly, the limbs of this doll are hollow.

Another company that did not last long was Mme. Rohmer of Paris. The company made dolls from 1857 to 1880. In 1857, Mme. Rohmer patented leather bodies with arms formed of rubber. In 1858, it patented a novel head fastening using a string that went through the head and body.

Schmitt & Sons, Emile Barrois and Belton

From 1863 to 1891, Schmitt & Sons of Paris used the body mark *SCH*, surrounded by a coat of arms. The working of porcelain shoulder heads for dolls and baby dolls was patented in 1877. In 1879, a patent was applied to entire bisque, jointed baby dolls. Bisque dolls and baby-doll heads were encased in wax by Schmitt & Sons. From 1879 to 1890, they made an unbreakable jointed doll called *Bébé Schmitt*.

Around 1880, Emile Barrois marked his dolls *EOB* on the shoulderplate.

Around the middle of the 19th century, Belton offered many types of dolls, including dolls with bald heads, without a pate. They had fixed eyes, closed mouth and a wood-jointed body.

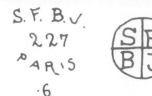

S. F. B. J.
227
PARIS
·6

SFBJ (Société Française de Fabrication de Bébés et Jouets), the French Society for the Manufacture of Baby Dolls and Toys, was based in Paris and Montreuil-sous-Bois from 1899 to 1925. It was a federation of French doll makers. Beautiful bisque character heads were made in Germany. Trademarks such as *Bébé Triomphe*, which means Baby Triumph, by Fleischmann & Bloedel, were registered, then made under SFBJ.

Schmitt & Sons of Paris made bisque heads, shoulder heads and baby dolls from 1863 to 1891.

R.4.D   R 5/0 D

Rabery & Delphieu of Paris made bisque heads, baby dolls, and walking and talking dolls from 1856 to 1898 (1899 in SFBJ). Bodies were wood composition, leather and other types.

BÉBÉ "LE PARISIEN"
MEDAILLE D'OR
PARIS

Neck mark of baby doll by Steiner.

EDEN-BÉBÉ

BÉBÉ TRIOMPHE

Fleischmann & Bloedel of Fuerth and Bavaria made bisque heads and walking and talking dolls from 1873 to 1914. They made dolls in Paris and became associated with SFBJ in 1899. Famous marks are *Eden Bébé* and *Bébé Triomphe*.

Doll Markings

On a painting, it is customary for the artist to sign his name or an abbreviation of his name. This is also done with dolls. The first line has the doll-maker's mark or the porcelain maker's, such as Jumeau or Heubach. Often an abbreviation, such as *AM*, was used. However, with dolls, you may find other markings.

Trademarks—Just as *Yoplait* is the name for a particular brand of yogurt, particular dolls were given names that were registered. *My Dream Baby, Walkure, Eden Bébé* and *Phenix* are examples of names given to dolls.

Trademark Symbols—In addition to the manufacturer's name, trademark or other marks, a doll might be marked with a particular symbol used by a doll-making firm, such as a star, rhombus, coat of arms or colophon.

Numbers and Letters—Dolls could also be marked with numbers. Numbers indicated the year of manufacture or the year in which the manufacturer's mold was first used. Forms were often used for years before being changed, so a doll marked *1896* might have been made in 1902. Painting can provide additional information in this case. Numbers designate a particular doll series or represent a patent number. Some numbers designate the size of the doll, but can refer to the model type.

Letters were used to indicate a doll's maker or to show where the doll was made. Kestner used the *Kestner Alphabet*, which was a letter-number combination, including the word *Germany*. The number indicated head size.

Registration Rights—Registration marks, such as *DRP, DRGM* and *dep*, without identification of the manufacturer, show the doll is protected with patents or the design is registered. The following abbreviations are common:

DRP—Abbreviation for *Deutsches Reichspatent*, which means German federal patent.

DRGM—Abbreviation for *Deutsches Reichsgebrauchsmuster*, which means German State Registered Design.

dep—Abbreviation for *deponiertes Geschmacksmuster*, which means German registration trademark.

DEP—Abbreviation for *deponiertes*.

Déposé—French version of *DEP*, above.

Reg.—Abbreviation for *registered* in English, which means the same as *dep*, above.

The Where, What and Who of Marks—If the back of the head or neck is marked, that marking is called a *neck mark*. Marks on shoulder-head dolls and other dolls are called *pet names*. Other markings were used on the sole of the foot of some dolls, such as Kewpies. However, bodies and eyes, such as those made by Steiner, were often marked separately. Jumeau and others did this with shoes as well.

In most cases, markings in the casting mold for the porcelain head resulted in the markings being cast along with the head. Indentations of letters, numerals or symbols found in the porcelain are not removable. Other types of stamped or written imprint marks could be removed chemically or lost through use. Adhesive labels or stamps were frequently used to mark bodies. In most cases, these marks did not pass the test of time.

Required Marks—Until 1890, manufacturers were not required to put visible marks on their products. As a result, up to that time, many porcelain makers had not marked their dolls. These early, often unmarked dolls—maker unknown—accounted for many of the most beautiful, rare dolls. There are many unmarked dolls from this period.

On August 23, 1887, England enacted a registration statute that acted as an international tariff agreement. Beginning in 1890, it required that all products exported to England or to other lands must identify their country of origin. At that point, it was sufficient to label the wrapper so dolls themselves no longer had to be marked. Later, exported products once again were incised directly with their country of origin, such as *Made in Germany, Made in France* or *France*.

Although there were attempts to avoid this type of marking, and oversights did occur, most dolls made after 1890 were marked with country of origin. Most included the manufacturer's mark, trademark or other identifying symbols.

Glossary of Doll Terms

This glossary offers quick access to information of interest to collectors of china, parian and bisque dolls. Information is concise to allow a beginning collector to learn quickly about doll types, changing materials, evolving techniques and markings.

Types of Porcelain

Bisque—Mat porcelain was used from 1860 to 1870 in France and Germany to make dolls that were painted after the first firing, then fired a second time. The second firing was about 1560F to 1650F (850C to 900C). The resulting bisque was more delicate than china. The term *bisque* originated from the French word *bisque* because porcelain, when fired with the coloring or paint, then baked a second time, resembles a biscuit.

China—Also called *glazed porcelain*, this hard-fired porcelain is glass fired to about 2500F (1400C). Lippert & Haas used china for doll heads. It was introduced at the 1845 Industry Fair in Vienna by Schlaggenwald, a porcelain manufacturer.

Parian—White-mat porcelain, which resembled Parian marble from the Isle of Paros, was created in 1842 in England. Two companies, W.T. Copeland and Minton & Co. of Staffordshire, found it useful for dolls. Parian dolls were made principally from 1850 to 1870.

Types of Dolls

ABC Dolls—Also called *teaching dolls*, these china shoulder-head dolls were made around 1905. Their cloth bodies are printed with letters of the alphabet, words and drawings. *Marion* and *Bertha* were two well-known dolls of this type. The best known ABC-doll maker was Butler Brothers of Thuringia and New York, from 1877 to 1925.

All-Bisque Dolls—Dolls made entirely of bisque.

Automatic Dolls, Running Dolls and Speaking Dolls—Highly complex running dolls were patented by Steiner in 1855. Around 1870, they became more popular, largely due to the many creations of Roullet & Decamps. See page 12. Speaking and music dolls were strongly influenced by Thomas Edison's invention of the phonograph in 1877.

Baby Dolls and Character Baby Dolls—Baby dolls and character baby dolls were popular from about 1909. Character baby dolls are distinguished by their realistic human facial expressions. In 1914, the first major breakthrough came when movable sleep eyes were produced. Around the turn of the century, Armand Marseille, a German manufacturer, produced a baby doll with a voice box. The speaking apparatus was inserted into the bisque head.

The *baby* of the French baby doll was often associated with a fantasy name like *Phénix*, *Mascotte*, *Metropole*, *Excelsior* and others. More often, names were linked to a company name, such as *Bébé Jumeau*, *Bébé Rabery* and *Bébé Bru*.

Eventually, German companies started using the nice-sounding term, *Bébé*. For example, Heinrich Handwerck registered the trademark *Bébé Cosmopolite*, and Max Handwerck registered *Bébé Elite*. Fleischmann & Bloedel used the name *Eden Bébé* from 1890 to 1925 in France and Germany. Fleischmann & Bloedel created *Bébé Triomphe*.

These trademark names were registered in 1913 for SFBJ, the alliance of French doll manufacturers. Although Fleischmann & Bloedel of Bavaria was a German doll maker, the company had a branch in Paris.

German baby dolls actually looked like babies but were intended mostly for adults. French baby dolls were made for children from 7 to 12 years old. When baby dolls came into demand, they replaced the then-popular lady dolls. See *Fashion Dolls*.

Bath Dolls—Bath dolls were cast in one piece of white china and pink bisque. They were made beginning around 1860. They had a hole in the back or head. Typical features included hands with closed fists, bent arms, sturdy bodies, and painted or painted, molded hair. Standing and sitting bath dolls were made. For information about *Frozen Charlies* and *Frozen Charlottes*, see *Miniature Dolls*.

Biedermeier Dolls—Biedermeier dolls were called *Victorian dolls*. These were made during the period of the classical Biedermeier, from 1815 to 1848. At the end of this period, dolls were made of china and parian "in the style of Biedermeier." See page 9. Around 1860, dolls were made of bisque. They can be recognized by a painted black spot on top of the head and no hair.

Bonnet Dolls—These dolls were made from 1840 to 1870. Heads were molded or cast in one piece along with bonnets, caps or similar head coverings.

Character Dolls—The term *character dolls* was coined in 1909 by German doll maker Kämmer & Reinhardt, who produced the first realistic human dolls. The impetus came from Marion Kaulitz, a member of a Munich artists' group who had produced the *Münchner Künstlerpuppe*, which means the Munich artist's doll, for a Munich exhibition in 1908. Following Kämmer & Reinhardt's lead, many other companies began producing character dolls and character baby dolls. Around 1910 in Germany, J.D. Kestner produced the doll *Das Wunderkind*, which means the wonder child, with three interchangeable bisque character heads. SFBJ character dolls have a good reputation.

Conventional Dolls—These are porcelain dolls not associated with other categories of doll types.

Dollhouse Dolls—Some dollhouse dolls are made of bisque.

Exotic Dolls—In this category are dolls of many races and skin colors, including Burmese, Japanese, Chinese, Indian and Negro. Dolls were clothed in their respective native dress and intended principally for export.

Produced primarily by German doll makers, these exotic dolls ranged in quality. Kestner, Simon & Halbig and Armand Marseille produced exceptionally good colored bisque. French doll makers Jumeau and Bru also made good-quality bisque dolls. The market for dolls of this type began to expand around 1890.

Fashion Dolls—Fashion dolls were called *Pandoras* in the 18th century. Dressed in the latest fashions, they were distributed throughout the world. After 1860, these dolls were outclassed by fashionably clothed Jumeau dolls with bisque heads. These fashion dolls represented French fashion internationally. However, other notable manufacturers were also represented by their *lady dolls* or *Parisiennes.*

Fortune-Teller Dolls—Usually on a stand, fortune-teller dolls were conversation pieces for adults and were popular around 1880. Under the coat of the Fortune Teller there were about 50 folded paper notes, on which fortunes were handwritten.

Googly Dolls—These dolls have exaggerated, large eyes that glance sideways. They are associated with character dolls as *caricature dolls*. The first reports of Googly dolls appeared in 1908, so it is assumed that is when they were first made. These dolls were followed by German production in many sizes. One extravagance was the Googly doll with crossed eyes created by Hermann Steiner of Germany.

In 1913, Kämmer & Reinhardt made two character dolls based on the *Max* and *Moritz* children's story characters. These dolls were not exclusively Googly dolls, but it is important to mention that they have interesting sleep and rascal eyes.

Half-Dolls—Half-dolls were called *tea dolls* and were popular from 1900 to 1930. Made of china or bisque, they were molded of one piece from the head to the waist. Typically, they measure between 1-1/2 and 4-3/4 inches (4cm and 12cm). The upper body was sewn on pin cushions or tea cozies.

Kewpie Dolls—These bisque dolls were designed primarily in America. They had large, roguish eyes, similar to Googly dolls, and made an impression with their cute expressions. The Kewpie patent was based on a design by Rose O'Neill, and the dolls were made in Germany by Kestner. Some were minidolls, while others were as large as 16-1/4 inches (41cm). The different poses and activities the dolls were involved in gave this generation of dolls variety. Kewpie dolls are mostly all-bisque dolls and are marked *Rose O'Neill* on the sole of the foot.

Knickknack Dolls—These were not play dolls. They were reserved as decorative accessories for a display case or mantelpiece. Knickknack dolls are diverse. Long mocked as useless, today they are regarded with great interest by collectors. They were made of china or bisque.

Marottes and Zouave Dolls—These have also been called *hand puppets* or *dolls on a stick*. Tiny bisque heads were fastened to a rotating stick, like puppets in a puppet theater. They are often harlequins or jesters wearing little bells. See page 7. Sometimes they have a music box under their costume.

Miniature Dolls—Most Marottes, dollhouse dolls, music-box dolls and smaller types of bath dolls, called *Frozen Charlottes* and *Frozen Charlies* by children, belong to this group. Frozen Charlottes and Frozen Charlies are based on an American folklore heroine around 1830 who froze to death during the night as a result of vanity.

Music-Box Dolls—These small dolls are mounted on music boxes that twirl around. Their heads were made of bisque. See page 6.

Nanking Dolls—Nanking dolls have china heads and fabric bodies. The body was made of a tight, almost-glossy polished cotton named after the Chinese city of Nanking.

Poor-People Dolls—Inexpensive dolls with bodies of pressed or stamped pulp were made in Germany from 1880 to 1884.

Portrait Dolls—These dolls were the fashion plates of the 19th century. Heads were modeled after real people, including children. This practice continued into the first decades of the 20th century.

Types of Doll Heads

Bald Head—This type of doll head has no opening on the top or back. It is dome-shaped and has painted hair and a wig. Glass eyes are inserted from below, through the neck opening. Among the French dolls, the Belton type is most noteworthy. Bald-head dolls are made of bisque, china and parian.

Cork Pate—A pate is the piece that fits in the open part of a bisque head. In French dolls, it is usually cork. In German dolls, it is cardboard.

Flange-Neck Head—Commonly found on baby dolls, this type of neck was made from about 1923. Body is cloth, and the neck is tapered, widening outward. The end is shaped like a ring. The body is attached, or tied on, through a number of holes in the end of the neck. The head may be almost impossible to turn, depending on how tightly it is tied on.

Hollow-Neck Head—The hollow-neck head was patented in 1919 by Johannes Gotthilf Dietrich. It is marked *Jgodi,* indicating it is a neckless head joined to the torso with a ball joint. A variation is a neckless head with an attachment similar to a socket joint. This fits into the top of a rounded neck fixture so the head can be moved easily.

Interchangeable Head—Some doll makers offered a doll set that contained several interchangeable bisque heads. An example is Kestner's *Das Wunderkind.*

Shoulder-Head Doll—This doll has head, neck, breast and shoulders in one piece. Because of this construction, the head does not move.

Swivel Head—Doll has a one-piece head and neck. The head-and-neck piece turns in the socket of the shoulder-plate or in a body. See page 26.

Turned-Head Doll—Head, neck and shoulders are one piece. The head is molded so it slightly tilts or turns to one side, but the head does *not* move.

Types of Doll Hair

Interchangeable Wig—The appearance of doll can be changed by using different wigs.

Human-Hair Wig—Hair is from a human head and is used on dolls with a realistic appearance. Hair is often painstakingly hand-tied.

Lambskin Wig—Made of the fleece of baby lambs, this type of wig is rare.

Mohair Wig—Originally hand-tied from Angora goat hair, which is fashioned into plaits. Wigs were machine made after about 1900.

Molded, Painted Hair—This is found on china, parian and bisque dolls. These dolls are readily classified by their hairstyles, such as Victorian.

Painted Hair—This was the simplest way to make hair. Painted hair was used mainly on china and parian dolls.

Types of Eyes, Eyebrows and Eyelashes

Eyebrows—Eyebrows were usually painted. On inexpensive dolls, they were simply drawn. For the highest-quality dolls, eyebrows were created with tiny strokes or feathery painting. Next came rippled eyebrows, then molded eyebrows that could be painted. For a short time, some bisque dolls had hair eyebrows, but these did not become popular.

Eyelashes—In addition to simple painted eyelashes consisting of decorative lines on the eyelids, doll eyelashes of hair, fur and fabric were used.

Fixed Glass Eyes—These were developed by Müller-Uri of Germany. Until 1835, irises of glass eyes were painted. Later, colored, extremely thin glass fibers were used to create the effect of an iris. This exciting new development was called *hollow glass eyes*, later *Parisian eyes*. When these glass eyes are well-made, they have a fascinating rayed iris.

Flirty Eyes—Invented around 1890 by Simon & Halbig, these eyes can be moved from side to side. A development from this type was movable sleep eyes, which opened and closed.

Intaglio Eyes—These are eyes with the iris and pupil incised or indented, then painted.

Movable Glass Sleep Eyes—By the 18th century, wire connectors were used on movable glass sleep eyes. Beginning in the 19th century, eyes were set in motion with an exterior pull string. Heinrich Stier, from Germany, patented movable glass sleep eyes in 1880. A lead pendulum acted as a counterweight inside the head. This caused the eyes to close automatically when the doll was moved from a vertical position to a horizontal position.

Painted Eyes—These are the simplest form of doll eyes and were the predecessors of glass eyes.

Paperweight Eyes—Paperweight eyes are called *glass-enamel eyes*. Speaking eyes were developed for Jumeau by Müller-Uri. See *Fixed Glass Eyes*. Another type of hand-blown eyes with colored inserts or multicolored glass similar to a paperweight was produced in Bristol, England after 1849. These eyes gave a previously unknown impression of depth.

Jumeau perfected this glass-blowing technique. With his glass-enamel eyes, he achieved the most beautiful, realistic artificial eyes ever produced.

The manufacturing process was complicated. Colored glass rods were heated to the melting point and blown to form a blue or brown iris around a black pupil. Then a piece of white opaque enamel was heated and poured to line the eyeball. The already-finished pupil was set in place in the hole in the eye socket. This painstaking process was finished with a thin coating of glass to give the eye a final gloss.

Paperweight or enameled glass eyes can be recognized by their depth. They are very humanlike when you look at them from the side.

Plastic Eyes—These eyes disfigure fine old porcelain dolls and are not appropriate to the style and type of doll. Try to exchange them for old glass eyes.

"Pseudo" Sleep Eyes—By placing the doll in a horizontal position, movable eyelids cover fixed eyeballs. These "pseudo" sleep eyes were patented by Jumeau in 1885.

Side-Glancing Eyes—Eyes, which are regular size, not oversize Googly eyes, are painted or set to the side. These eyes were introduced in 1913 along with the merry Googly dolls. Staring eyes are similar.

Types of Doll Mouths

Bouche Fermé—Among French dolls, this is the designation for a *closed mouth*.

Clenched Mouth—Bisque dolls with tightly closed, or clenched, mouths were uncommon. An example of this type is Simon & Halbig's No.1833 doll.

Closed Mouth—Most bisque dolls have a closed mouth because this was the easiest way to make them. Today, closed-mouth dolls are among the most sought after, most expensive dolls when compared to those with an open mouth. The shape and coloring of the mouth is critical to the strength of its expression.

Open Mouth—Steiner dolls with an open mouth usually have molded or cut teeth above or below, rarely above *and* below. The shape of the mouth and quality of the painting vary. A mouth with a strong expression was often painted twice and contoured with emphasized curves.

Open-Closed Mouth—This type of mouth has tongue and teeth molded and painted to form the impression of an open mouth. There is no actual opening into the inside of the mouth. Doll mouths that have an unpainted portion between the upper and lower lips are called *open-closed*.

Open Mouth with Movable Tongue—This type of doll could move its tongue as a result of an invention in 1925 by Franz Schmidt & Co.

Pouty Mouth—Pouty mouths are found on bisque dolls, especially German character dolls. An example is *Hans* and *Gretchen*, No.114 of Kämmer & Reinhardt. For more information about these dolls, see HPBooks' *Treasury of German Dolls*, by Lydia Richter.

Types of Doll Bodies

Body Combinations—It was common to make dolls from a combination of different materials. For example, a leather body might have a bisque head and wood or porcelain arms. These combinations, including arms made of Celluloid and other synthetic materials, were common.

Cloth Bodies—Dolls with cloth bodies have a past rich in tradition. Dolls were filled with wool, horsehair, seaweed, sawdust and other materials. The cloth body of the *Nanking Doll* was made of a dense, almost smooth, cotton fabric, which was named after the Chinese city Nanking. Oilcloth was used for bodies.

Composition Bodies—Pulp is the fiber left after paper is made. It was added to lime, paste, chalk, sand and other materials to make composition. Composition is the most common substance used for bisque doll bodies.

Leather Bodies—Goatskin was used for some leather bodies. Generally, it was white. However, occasionally it was colored pink. On some French leather bodies, gussets were sewn at the arms and legs to enhance movement. Kestner used this technique in Germany. Leather-jointed bodies with different types of connections and bindings, such as wire frames inside the doll, were developed. Some joints were riveted, while others, such as hips, were nailed.

Papier-Mâché Bodies—Papier-mâché bodies were first made by hand, then later by machine. Bodies were pressed into half forms. Papier-mâché was strong. Limbs were hollow but fingers had to be cast in solid pieces and were more delicate and susceptible to damage.

Porcelain Bodies—All-bisque dolls are those made entirely of porcelain from head to foot. Included in this group are dollhouse dolls, bath dolls, knickknack dolls and others.

Sitting-Baby Bodies—Based on the image of a 6-month-old infant, these dolls have composition bodies with bent limbs. Bent knees made possible the natural sitting position of baby dolls. They became popular around 1909.

Standing-Baby Bodies—This composition body type was made after 1912. It was based on the image of a 2-year-old child. This baby doll could only stand.

Standing-Sitting-Baby Bodies—This baby body was made so the baby doll could sit and stand.

Stiff-Jointed Bodies—These bodies had only four joints. Although they were able to stand, this body was a regression, in terms of movement. Stiff-jointed bodies became available around 1890.

Toddler Bodies—Toddler bodies were short and stocky and made of composition. In one variety of toddler body, upper legs are short so knees are higher. This avoids showing the bend of the knee when the doll wore then-fashionable short dresses.

Wood Bodies—Wood has always been suitable for making doll bodies because it is a clean, natural material. Wood bodies and dolls of wood were often made in heavily wooded districts, such as those found in Germany. Wood-jointed bodies were made almost from the beginning.

Wood-Composition Ball-and-Socket Jointed Bodies—Doll torso, legs and arms bound to wood balls allowed doll joints to move in all directions. Eight- or 10-jointed bodies were most common, but there were 12-jointed bodies. French doll maker Bru invented the ball-and-socket joint and patented it in 1869. Heinrich Stier used this type of body in Germany in 1880.

Other Special Terms and Concepts

Advertising Jingles—Even in the early 1900s, the doll industry recognized the commercial value of advertising jingles. For example, a translation of one jingle by Kley & Hahn for the company's two-faced doll, patented in 1912 was:

> When she is awake, she laughs.
> If you turn her little head around,
> Then the little girl will cry.

Firing Cracks—These cracks result from firing porcelain. Generally, they are harmless and do not diminish the doll's worth significantly. But this is true only if the cracks do not go through the face or present danger for greater damage.

Gibson Girl—Based on drawings by American Charles Dana Gibson, these bisque portrait dolls are shapely, womanly dolls.

Hairline Cracks—Often, hairline cracks in a bisque head considerably reduce the value of a doll—especially if professional restoration is done. The degree of value loss depends on whether the crack goes through the face and how big it is.

Labeling—Stick-on labels were commonly used to mark doll bodies, although often a stamp was used.

Marked—This is the industry expression for marking dolls on the back of the head, the nape of the neck or the shoulder head. See page 21.

Pressers—Doll-industry workers who pressed composition into the required shapes were called *pressers*.

Talking Head—Dolls with a talking head were made by Amberg & Hergershausen in 1925. Dolls said a short rhyme explaining it would speak when cheeks were squeezed and that it would not break if dropped.

Unmarked—Before 1890, no law required dolls to be marked. Then, a trademark law required that a distinguishing mark indicating the country of origin had to be written on the packing material or the article. As a result, doll makers often added their firm name or commercial mark. See page 21.

Bisque Swivel-Head Dolls

Swivel-head dolls have a one-piece head and neck that turns in the socket of the shoulderplate. The conical, tapered neck runs directly into the doll body. Two-part bodies are made up of the head-neck piece and the body. Limbs are extra pieces.

Doll standing in field is shown wearing lace hat in close-up photo on opposite page and is described below.

Belton

Bisque, Belton, 19-3/4 inches (50cm). Made around 1885, swivel-head doll has pink cheeks. Fixed, blue paperweight eyes have rayed irises, outlined eyelashes and painted eyebrows. Mouth is open-closed, with emphasized curves, and ears are pierced. Composition body has 10 joints. Doll wears old wig. Costume is original.

Bru

Bisque, Bru, 27-1/2 inches (70cm), marked *BRU Jne. R12.* Made around 1890, swivel-head doll has pink cheeks. Dark-brown, almond-shaped, glass sleep eyes have rayed irises, grooved eyelid borders above outlined black eyelashes and dark-brown, feathered eyebrows. Slightly open mouth, with emphasized curves, has four teeth on top, and ears are pierced. Wig is new human hair. Composition body has 10 joints. New costume is made from old material. Doll has been slightly restored at the forehead. Doll is shown in close-up photo on opposite page without hat, wearing different costume and wig.

Functioning, hand-cranked sewing machine with flower design, 8-3/4x7-1/2 inches (22x19cm). Made around 1920. Doll is shown in close-up photo on opposite page.

Denamur

Bisque, Denamur, 17 inches (43cm), marked *E 6 D DEPOSÉ*. Made around 1890, swivel-head doll has light-pink, tinted cheeks. Fixed, cornflower-blue paperweight eyes have painted eyelashes and dark-brown, feathered eyebrows. Slightly open mouth, with emphasized curves, has four teeth on top, and ears are pierced. Wig is new light-blond, human hair. Composition body has 10 joints. New costume is made from old fabric.

Fleischmann & Bloedel

Bisque, Fleischmann & Bloedel, 20-1/2 inches (52cm),
marked *Eden-Bébé Paris Gr.9*. Made around 1898,
swivel-head doll is delicately tinted. Fixed, gray-blue
paperweight eyes have rayed irises, painted eyelashes and
finely outlined, light-brown eyebrows. Open mouth, with
emphasized curves, has six teeth on top, and ears are
pierced. Wig is new human hair. The Bébé Jumeau body
has a voice box, stamped *VRAI Modèle Fabr. Jumeau*. New
costume is made from old fabric. Doll is shown on opposite
page wearing different costume, without hat.

Teddy bear, 15-3/4 inches (40cm).

Fleischmann & Bloedel

Bisque, Fleischmann & Bloedel, 21-1/4 inches (54cm), marked *Eden-Bébé Paris I*. Made around 1892, swivel-head doll is light pink with rose-tinted cheeks. Black-brown paperweight eyes have painted eyelashes and emphasized eyebrows. Mouth is closed, and ears are pierced. Wig is old, red-brown human hair. Composition stiff-jointed body has four joints. Costume is original.

Gaultier

Bisque, Gaultier, 25-1/2 inches (65cm), marked *F.G.* Made around 1885, swivel-head doll has delicate, pink-tinted cheeks. Fixed, brown paperweight eyes have painted eyelashes and feathered eyebrows. Mouth is closed, with emphasized curves, and ears are pierced. Wig is old human hair. Composition body has 10 joints. Fingernails are red-lacquered. Costume is old.

Doll in pink dress is shown wearing white-lace dress without beads in close-up photo on opposite page and is described below.

Jullien

Bisque, Jullien, 15-3/4 inches (40cm), marked *JJ*. Made around 1885, swivel-head doll has delicate pink cheeks and dimpled chin. Dark-blue paperweight eyes have black outline, painted eyelashes and painted, brown eyebrows. Open, pale rose-colored mouth, with emphasized curves, has five teeth on top. Ears are pierced, and doll wears old pierced earrings. Wig is new human hair. Composition stiff-jointed body has four joints. New costume is made from old fabric.

Tin-plate coffee mill, 2-3/4 inches
(7cm) high, was made around 1910.

Lecomte (Leconte) & Alliot

Bisque, Lecomte (Leconte) & Alliot, 22-1/2 inches (57cm),
marked *LC* and *Anker*. Made around 1880, swivel-head
doll has brown-rose tinted cheeks. Brown glass sleep eyes
have painted eyelashes and painted eyebrows. Open
mouth has five teeth on top, and ears are pierced. Wig is
brown human hair. Composition body has 10 joints.
Costume is new.

Doll standing amid flowers is shown in close-up photo on opposite page and is described below.

Rabery & Delphieu

Bisque, Rabery & Delphieu, 19-3/4 inches (50 cm), marked *R.2.D.* Made around 1892, swivel-head doll has intensely colored cheeks. Golden-brown paperweight eyes have painted eyelashes and thickly feathered, dark-brown eyebrows. Mouth is closed. Wig is dark-brown human hair. Composition jointed body has 10 joints. Body is stamped *Bébé L'universal-Incassable*, which means *unbreakable universal baby doll*. Old costume is made from tulle.

Doll on left is German doll *Revalo* made by Ohlhaver Brothers. For information, see HPBooks' *Treasury of German Dolls*, also by Lydia Richter. Doll on right is shown in close-up photo on opposite page and is described below.

Henri Rostal

Bisque, Rostal, 22-3/4 inches (58cm), marked *30 MON TRÉSOR 9*. Made around 1890, swivel-head doll has orange-red cheeks. Fixed, blue eyes have rayed irises, painted eyelashes and strongly outlined, dark-brown eyebrows. Mouth is open, with four teeth on top, and ears are pierced. Wig is new mohair. Partially restored composition body has 10 joints. Costume is typical Jumeau, made of old material.

Steiner

Bisque, Steiner, 8-3/4 inches (22cm), marked *J. Steiner.*
BTE 3. GDE Paris FRE A 1. Made around 1895,
swivel-head doll has pink cheeks. Fixed, sky-blue
paperweight eyes have rayed irises and brown eyebrows.
Mouth is closed, and ears are pierced. Wig is new mohair.
Composition body has eight joints. Costume is old.

Doll with silver bird is shown wearing hat in close-up photo on opposite page and is described below.

Unis France

Bisque, Unis France, 23-3/4 inches (60cm), marked *Unis France 71301149*. Made around 1923, swivel-head doll has rosy-red cheeks and dimpled chin. Brown glass sleep eyes have painted eyelashes below, hair eyelashes above and brown feathered eyebrows. Open mouth has four teeth on top. Wig is new mohair. Composition body has 10 joints. Costume is new.

Collection of doll shoes, made between 1885 and 1910.

Maker unknown

Bisque, maker unknown, 25-1/2 inches (65cm), marked *32-315.* Swivel-head doll has strongly pink-tinted cheeks. Fixed, dark-brown glass eyes have painted eyelashes and painted eyebrows. Mouth is closed, and ears are pierced. Wig is new human hair. French composition body has 10 joints. New costume is made from old fabric.

Bisque Swivel-Head on Shoulderplate Doll

This type of doll has a movable head. The head-neck piece is seated in a separate section, which is a shoulderplate. The shoulderplate is separate from the body and bound to it with stitches or glue. Three-part bodies are made up of the head, breast-shoulderplate and body. Limbs are extra pieces.

Maker unknown

Bisque, presumably Gaultier. Made around 1880, doll with swivel-head on shoulderplate has delicate pink-tinted cheeks. Fixed, brown eyes have rayed irises, painted eyelashes and painted eyebrows. Mouth is closed, with emphasized curves, and ears are pierced. Wig is old mohair. Doll has pinch-waist cloth body with bisque lower arms. Her original wedding dress is silk. The shoulderplate part is damaged.

Bisque Shoulder-Head Dolls

The head, neck, breast and shoulders are one piece in bisque shoulder-head dolls, as shown on far right on the opposite page. Because of this construction, the head does not move.

Maker unknown

Above and left on opposite page: Bisque, presumably Madame Rohmer, 18-1/2 inches (47cm). Made around 1875, fashion doll with swivel head on shoulderplate has strongly tinted cheeks. Fixed, blue glass eyes have painted eyelashes and outlined eyebrows. Small mouth is closed, with emphasized curves, and ears are pierced. Wig is original mohair. Body is finely worked leather. Joints are wood with leather pulled over them, and arms are bisque. Costume is original.

On right: Bisque, presumably Gaultier, 17-1/4 inches (44cm). Made around 1870, shoulder-head fashion doll has rosy cheeks. Fixed, cobalt-blue eyes have outlined eyelashes and painted eyebrows. Small mouth is closed, with emphasized curves, and ears are pierced. Wig is original mohair. Lady-doll body is made of kid leather.

The Jumeau Gallery

Emile Jumeau, called the *King of Dolls*, created some of the most beautiful dolls ever made. The glass-enameled paperweight eyes, painting and porcelain were as charming as their costumes. See page 13.

Jumeau

Bisque, Jumeau, 9-3/4 inches (25cm), head marked *Déposé Tête Jumeau, BTE S.G.D. 1.* Made around 1890, swivel-head doll has black artist's marks and delicate rose-tinted cheeks. Fixed, violet-blue paperweight eyes have rayed irises, painted eyelashes and tinted eyebrows. Mouth is closed, with emphasized curves, and ears are pierced. Wig is original mohair on cork base. Composition body has 10 joints. Body is stamped *Bébé Jumeau Diplômé d'Honneur.* New costume is made of old material. Doll is shown on opposite page with different hat.

Doll in profile is shown full-face in close-up photo on opposite page and is described below.

Jumeau

Bisque, Jumeau, 18-1/2 inches (47cm). Made around 1890, swivel-head doll has artist's marks and delicate, slightly tinted cheeks. Fixed, sky-blue paperweight eyes have rayed irises, painted dark-brown eyelashes and painted eyebrows. Mouth is closed, with emphasized curves. Ears are pierced and have coral earrings. Wig is original light-blond mohair on cork base. Original Bébé-Jumeau body has 10 joints. New Jumeau costume is made from old silk and lace.

Symphonium is German-made, hand-cranked music box using 5-3/4-inch (14.5cm) steel discs. Made in 1902.

Jumeau

Bisque, Jumeau, 16-1/2 inches (42cm), marked —5. Made around 1890, swivel-head doll is almost white, similar to parian, which makes it rare. Dark-blue paperweight eyes have rayed irises, slightly suggested eyelashes and strongly outlined eyebrows. Open mouth, with emphasized curves, has six teeth. Body is typical Bébé Jumeau. Old costume is made from red velvet.

Doll with birds is shown in close-up photo on opposite page and is described below.

Jumeau

Bisque, Jumeau, 20-1/2 inches (52cm), marked 8. Made around 1885, swivel-head doll has slightly tinted, light-pink cheeks. Glass sleep eyes have dark-blue rayed irises, cloth eyelashes with finely painted lashes completely encircling the eye, and strongly outlined eyebrows. Open mouth, with emphasized curves, has six teeth on top, and ears are pierced. Wig is old human hair. Typical Bébé Jumeau body has speaking mechanism and pullstring. New Jumeau costume is made from old silk and lace.

Three-wheeled wood doll carriage is black lacquer with red and yellow stripes and was made around 1870. Doll in carriage is shown in close-up photo on opposite page and is described below.

Jumeau

Bisque, Jumeau, 20-1/2 inches (52cm), marked *1907.9*. Made around 1910, swivel-head doll has brown-pink tinted cheeks and chin dimple. Fixed, brown paperweight eyes have painted eyelashes and strongly tinted dark-brown eyebrows. Slightly open mouth, with emphasized curves, has teeth on top, and ears are pierced. Wig is new human hair. Bébé Jumeau body has 10 joints. New costume is made from old silk, and glass pearls are sewn on.

Doll in blue fantasyland is shown in close-up photo on opposite page and is described below.

Jumeau

Bisque, Jumeau, 23-3/4 inches (60cm), marked 8. Made around 1900, swivel-head doll has rose-tinted cheeks. Sky-blue glass sleep eyes have rayed irises, painted eyelashes and strongly tinted eyebrows. Slightly open, outlined mouth has six teeth on top, and ears are pierced. Wig is new light-blond human hair. Composition body has straight limbs and eight joints. New costume is made of old taffeta silk from an original Jumeau pattern. Stockings are hand knit. Doll walks with moving mechanism.

Jumeau

Bisque, Jumeau, 22-3/4 inches (58cm), marked *Tête Jumeau*. Made around 1890, swivel-head doll has delicately tinted cheeks. Fixed, brown paperweight eyes have painted eyelashes and painted dark-brown eyebrows. Open mouth, with emphasized curves, has six teeth on top, and ears are pierced. Wig is hand-tied, red-blond human hair. Typical Bébé Jumeau body has talking mechanism and drawstring. Costume is original Jumeau bridal dress made of cream-colored satin silk. Underclothing is original. Cream-colored silk shoes, lace stockings, garters and kid gloves are original. Veil is made of net lace with wax-flower crown and bridal bouquet.

Portrait Dolls

As a rule, dolls are called *portrait dolls* when they have heads modeled after known personalities.

Doll is shown in close-up photo on opposite page and is described below.

Jumeau

Bisque, Jumeau, 15-3/4 inches (40cm), marked with artist's marks. Doll is called *Portrait Jumeau*. Made around 1890, swivel-head doll has rose-tinted cheeks. Fixed, sky-blue paperweight eyes have rayed irises with black rims, painted eyelashes and painted light-brown eyebrows. Mouth is closed, with emphasized curves, and ears are pierced. Wig is light-blond original mohair on cork base. Original Bébé Jumeau body has 10 joints. New Jumeau-style dress is made from old silk and lace.

DEP Jumeau

For a while, Jumeau heads were made in Germany at a lower cost. These heads were marked *DEP*, as explained on page 18. If a DEP-marked doll has a Jumeau body, it generally can be concluded it is a *DEP Jumeau*.

Jumeau

Bisque, Jumeau, head apparently made by Simon & Halbig (Germany) for Jumeau, 27-1/2 inches (70cm), marked *DEP No. 12.* Swivel-head doll has brown-pink tinted cheeks and chin dimple. Blue paperweight eyes have rayed irises, painted eyelashes and strongly outlined brown eyebrows. Open mouth has six teeth on top, and ears are pierced. Wig is old hand-tied, blond human hair. Body is typical Bébé Jumeau. New costume is made from old fabric. Shoes are old leather shoes.

Kiss in the Ring 18th century

lies Graces 19th century

Plush lamb was made by Steiff around 1949. Lamb has ear clip, which is famous Steiff trademark. Doll sitting on lamb is shown without her brooch in close-up photo on opposite page and is described below.

Jumeau

Bisque, Jumeau, head made in Germany for Jumeau, 14-1/2 inches (37cm), marked *DEP 5*. Made around 1900, swivel-head doll has delicate pink cheeks and dimpled chin. Blue sleep eyes have rayed irises, top eyelashes of cloth, painted lower lashes and molded, outlined light-brown eyebrows. Open mouth has four teeth on top, and ears are pierced. Original wig is blond mohair. Typical Bébé Jumeau body. Costume is new Jumeau style made from old silk and lace.

Archery 16th century

"Pall Mall"

Jumeau

Bisque, Jumeau, head made in Germany for Jumeau, 15 inches (38cm), marked *DEP 3*. Made around 1900, swivel-head doll has delicate pink cheeks. Dark-blue glass sleep eyes have rayed irises, with top eyelashes of cloth, painted lower eyelashes and molded, outlined eyebrows. Small, open mouth has four teeth, and ears are pierced. Earrings of brass wire and glass are original. Wig is hand-tied original mohair on cork base. Composition body is typical Bébé Jumeau. New costume includes original shoes and stockings. Doll is shown on opposite page wearing different dress.

Football
played
in the Strand
18 th century

Porcelain cup with doll's head,
2-1/4 inches (6cm) high, made
around 1900.

Jumeau

Bisque, Jumeau, head presumably by Simon & Halbig
(Germany) for Jumeau, 19-3/4 inches (50cm), marked *DEP
8*. Swivel-head doll has pink-tinted cheeks. Fixed blue
eyes have brown irises, painted eyelashes and molded
eyebrows. Slightly open mouth has four teeth on top, and
ears are pierced. Original wig is brown mohair. Jumeau
body has 10 joints. Original costume is decorated with old
lace.

Tilting at the
Quintain at Offham
15th century

Handmade bicycle of tin-plate, 9-3/4 inches (25cm) high.

Jumeau

Bisque, Jumeau, head presumably by Simon & Halbig (Germany) for Jumeau, 19-3/4 inches (50cm), marked *DEP 8*. Made around 1890, swivel-head doll has pink-tinted cheeks. Fixed, brown glass eyes have painted eyelashes and molded eyebrows. Slightly open mouth has four teeth on top, and ears are pierced. Wig is original brown mohair. Jumeau composition body has 10 joints. Original cotton costume is decorated with old lace.

Hunt the Slipper
17th century

Jumeau

Bisque, Jumeau, made in Germany for Jumeau, 15-3/4 inches (40cm), marked *DEP 6*. Swivel-head doll has brown-pink cheeks and dimpled chin. Fixed, brown paperweight eyes have eyelashes painted on bottom lid, and molded, painted eyebrows. Open mouth, with emphasized curves, has four teeth on top, and ears are pierced. Wig is old hand-tied human hair. Bébé Jumeau composition body has voice apparatus and drawstring mechanism. New costume is made from old silk and lace.

Sword &
Buckler Play

13th century

Bob Apple   13th

Société Française de Fabrication de Bébés et Jouets, SFBJ

(French Society for the Manufacture of Baby Dolls and Toys)

The difficult struggle for survival among German doll manufacturers caused doll makers in France to band together to form the SFBJ. See page 19. Produced under this neck mark, these interesting character dolls were especially noteworthy.

SFBJ

Bisque, SFBJ, 19-3/4 inches (50cm), marked *SFBJ 60/Paris No. 3*. Made around 1910, swivel-head doll has light-pink tinted cheeks. Blue glass sleep eyes have rayed irises with black rims, painted eyelashes and painted eyebrows. Wig is new dark-brown human hair. Stiff-limbed body is made of papier-mâché. Costume is new. Doll is shown on opposite page in a different costume.

Original Montanari dress.

SFBJ

Bisque, SFBJ, 17 inches (43cm), marked *SFBJ 60 Paris 2/0*. Made around 1910, swivel-head doll has orange-brown cheeks. Black glass sleep eyes have painted eyelashes and light-brown painted eyebrows. Open mouth has four teeth on top. Wig is new human hair with dark-auburn corkscrew curls. Body is papier-mâché and wood, with 10 joints. Costume is made from old material.

Doll sitting in tree is shown in different hat and hair arrangement in close-up photo on opposite page and is described below.

SFBJ

Bisque, SFBJ, 23-3/4 inches (60cm), marked *SFBJ 301, Paris 22*. Made around 1915, swivel-head doll has brown-pink tinted cheeks. Black-brown, almond-shaped glass sleep eyes have painted black eyelashes and brown eyebrows. Open mouth, with emphasized curves, has four teeth on top, and ears are pierced. Wig is old dark-brown human hair. Composition body has eight joints. Costume is old.

Character Dolls
and Character Baby Dolls

Character dolls first became popular in 1909, mostly in Germany. SFBJ contributed beautiful dolls to this genre.

SFBJ

Bisque, SFBJ, 17 inches (43cm), both marked *SFBJ 236 Paris*. Made around 1910, swivel-head dolls have rosy cheeks. Dark-blue glass sleep eyes have top eyelashes of hair, painted lower eyelashes and painted eyebrows. Open-closed mouth has molded tongue and two molded teeth on top. Composition toddler body is called *Lachende Jumeau*, which means Laughing Jumeau. Boy doll on opposite page wears original mohair wig and original sailor costume. Girl doll above has new mohair wig. New costume is made from old organdy, and includes an old garland, old shoes and old stockings.

Mechanical, Semiautomatic and Automatic Dolls

Many mechanical and automatic dolls were made and some could talk. Of particular note were dolls made by Steiner. See pages 18 and 19. But Bru, page 16, Jumeau, pages 17 and 18, and others, successfully made these doll types.

Automatic dolls were often made by technically oriented companies not otherwise involved with the doll industry. Roullet & Decamps was one company.

Collecting automatic dolls is a special field that arouses great enthusiasm among collectors with technical interests. Not all doll collectors like automatic dolls. They find them heavy, stiff and uncuddly.

Chain drive inside body pulls spring mechanism that sets wheels in motion on soles of this walking doll.

Fleischmann & Bloedel

Bisque, Fleischmann & Bloedel, 23-3/4 inches (60cm), marked *DEP*. Made around 1895, swivel-head doll has brown-tinted cheeks and chin dimple. Blue glass sleep eyes have rayed irises, top eyelashes of silk thread, painted lower lashes and strongly molded eyebrows. Slightly open mouth, with emphasized curves, has four teeth on top, and ears are pierced. Wig is original red mohair. Composition body and legs are one piece, and arms have six joints. New costume is made from old material. This semiautomatic walking doll was called *Eden Bébé*.

Shuttle-cock
15 th century

Steiner

Bisque, Steiner, 25-1/2 inches (65cm), marked *A 15 Paris*
"Le Parisien." Made around 1890, doll has a swivel head.
Fixed violet paperweight glass eyes have rayed irises,
painted eyelashes and strongly tinted eyebrows. Slightly
open mouth, with emphasized curves, has eight teeth, and
ears are pierced. Wig is original light-blond, hand-tied
mohair. Wood composition body has 10 joints. Costume is
original silk dress with bonnet. White fingernails are
molded. This semiautomatic walking doll has a walking
mechanism and voice box, with a key on the side to make
it run. Doll is stamped *"Le Petit Parisien"* Bébé Steiner
Gold Medaille d'Or Paris 1889.

Marquis Fumeur—Smoking Marquis
Using a beautiful Jumeau head, Roullet & Decamps created an elegant, versatile automatic doll. A spring mechanism is built into the body and drives toothed wheels, rods and a bellows, see page 17. This raises the doll's right hand, bringing a burning cigarette to its mouth. Through a rubber tube in the arm, the doll takes a puff of smoke, then lowers his right arm and raises his glasses to his eyes with his left arm. When he lowers his left arm, he exhales smoke from his mouth. This is made possible by the bellows automatically pressing together inside the body. The smoker also raises and lowers his head. A music box built into the base plays a melody.

Jumeau

Bisque, Jumeau head with Roullet & Decamps adaptation, 23-3/4 inches (60cm), marked *Déposé Tête Jumeau No. 5,* including artist's marks. Made around 1888, swivel-head doll has pink-tinted cheeks. Cornflower-blue paperweight eyes have rayed irises, outlined eyelashes and strongly tinted eyebrows. Slightly open mouth has emphasized curves, and ears are pierced. Wig is original mohair. Automatic body is made of wood and metal. Original silk costume is in the style of the 18th century. This rare smoking, automatic doll has various movement mechanisms and a music box.

Dick Whittington's Parlour

Aldgate

Ye Olde Streete Cries

Butchers-row.

Maker unknown

Bisque, presumably Steiner, doll 9-3/4 inches (25cm), doll and cycle, 14-1/2 inches (37cm), marked 2/0. Made around 1890. Head and arms are bisque, and body is wood. Fixed glass eyes are dark brown. Mouth is closed. Wig is white-blond mohair. Original silk clothing includes gold lace. Doll rides high-wire cycle. When hand crank is turned, doll pedals, setting wheel in motion, to run on wire. Balance is achieved with hanging pendulum.

Reproductions and Forgeries of Bisque Dolls

More reproductions and forgeries have become available. True reproductions are marked so their modern maker is discernible. In forgeries, either the mark of the original manufacturer is put on without a modern addition or no mark is indicated at all.

Bru Reproduction

Bisque, Bru Reproduction, 19 inches (48cm), marked *Bru Jne. "Butler Repro 100/1980."* Swivel-head doll has rosy cheeks. Blue paperweight eyes, outlined in black, have rayed irises, painted eyelashes and painted eyebrows. Closed mouth has emphasized lines. Wig is new mohair. New cloth body has bisque lower arms and legs. New costume is made from old silk and tulle lace.

Old embroidered fan made of ivory and silk around 1910. It is 7 inches (18cm).

Bru Forgery

Bisque, Bru Forgery, 16-1/2 inches (42cm), marked *BRU J.*
Swivel-head doll has delicate rose cheeks. Glass eyes are
dark blue. Closed mouth has emphasized lines, and ears
are pierced. Wig is new blond mohair. New cloth body has
bisque lower arms and hands. New costume is made from
old material. Doll is considered a forgery because it has no
modern artist's marking.

Doll standing amid flowers is shown wearing different hat in close-up photo on opposite page and is described below.

Steiner Reproduction

Bisque, Steiner Reproduction, 17-3/4 inches (45cm), marked *A 9/F.G. (Friedl Groebl) Reproduktion 1980.* Swivel-head doll is made of silky-smooth bisque. Old hand-blown glass eyes have painted eyelashes and painted eyebrows. Closed mouth has emphasized curves. Wig is new mohair. New handworked leather body has molded bust. Lower arms are molded, and hands and feet are bisque. New costume is made from old material.

Elegant doll umbrella made of black lace worked on white silk. Handle is hand-carved ivory.

Maker unknown

Bisque, maker unknown, presumably French, 20-3/4 inches (53cm). Swivel-head doll is made of unusual soap-smooth, almost-silky, light-pink tinted bisque, with rosy cheeks. Fixed, brown paperweight eyes have painted eyelashes and painted eyebrows. Mouth is closed, with emphasized curves, and ears are pierced. Wig is old human hair on recently cut old-cork bald head. Body is old AM body. Costume is old.

Rabery & Delphieu R. & D., made around 1892

Bru J12, made around 1890

Fleischmann & Bloedel *Eden Bébé*, made around 1892

Jumeau 749/3/0, made around 1900

Bru Reproduction, *Butler*, made in 1980

Bru Forgery

Doll Scenes in Paintings, Engravings and Illustrations

A major increase in demand for dolls occurred between 1880 and 1920. During this period, artists dedicated much of their work to doll or child-and-doll themes.

Oil paintings, watercolors, engravings, and book and magazine illustrations tell much about the lifestyle, fashions and hairstyles of this period. Collectables are witnesses of the past, reflecting a part of a culture's history.

Oil painting from southern Germany, painted around 1890

Watercolor, painted around 1910

Christmas, a colored wood cut from *The Graphic*, made in 1881

Bridge Works, from painting by K. Raupp

To America! from painting by R. Hirth

The Doll as a Photographer's Prop

Childrens' fears of the "big magic box under the black cloth" were reduced considerably when they were photographed with their dolls. Photographs of this type are an excellent record of dolls and the times.

Doll Scenes on Post Cards and Other Collectable Cards

Children in adult settings were shown with dolls on photo post cards, which were mailed around the world. Children and dolls were a well-loved motif on painted post cards and other collectable cards.

Collection of cards illustrated with dolls

Bonne Année

Christmas cards showing doll scenes

Doll Manufacturing

These illustrations from the magazine *Illustrierte Welt* (*Illustrated World*) of 1888 show some of the doll-making process.

Preparing and assembling parts of jointed dolls

Lacquering bodies

Applying hair

Painting dolls

Trimming doll heads

Index

7.42397830329